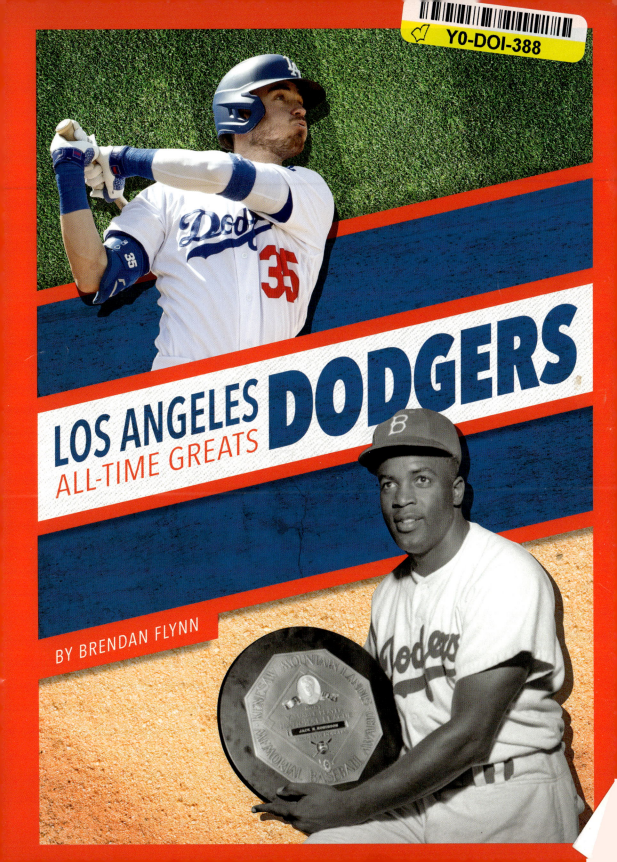

LOS ANGELES DODGERS

ALL-TIME GREATS

BY BRENDAN FLYNN

Book design by Jake Slavik
Cover design by Jake Slavik

Photographs ©: Sam Gangwer/AP Images, cover (top), 1 (top); Marty Lederhandler/AP Images, cover (bottom), 1 (bottom); AP Images, 4, 10, 12; David Durochik/AP Images, 6; Louis Lopez/Cal Sport Media/AP Images, 9; Bettmann/Getty Images, 13; Rusty Kennedy/AP Images, 14; John Swart/AP Images, 16; B Bennett/Getty Images Sport Classic/Getty Images, 18; Kiyoshi Mio/Icon Sportswire/AP Images, 20; Red Line Editorial, 22

Press Box Books, an imprint of Press Room Editions.

ISBN
978-1-63494-292-8 (library bound)
978-1-63494-310-9 (paperback)
978-1-63494-346-8 (epub)
978-1-63494-328-4 (hosted ebook)

Library of Congress Control Number: 2020913893

Distributed by North Star Editions, Inc.
2297 Waters Drive
Mendota Heights, MN 55120
www.northstareditions.com

Printed in the United States of America
012021

ABOUT THE AUTHOR

Brendan Flynn is a San Francisco resident and an author of numerous children's books. In addition to writing about sports, Flynn also enjoys competing in triathlons, Scrabble tournaments, and chili cook-offs.

TABLE OF CONTENTS

KOUFAX
32

CHAPTER 1
PITCHERS

The Dodgers have played in the National League (NL) since 1890. They began playing in Brooklyn, New York. Their name comes from the streetcars that traveled on the local roads. People had to avoid them as they crossed the streets. They were called "trolley dodgers."

The team moved to Los Angeles in 1958. They didn't win a lot in Brooklyn. But they became a great team in their new home. One reason was outstanding pitching from one of the best left-handers ever, **Sandy Koufax**.

Koufax won three NL Cy Young Awards. He also was the NL Most Valuable Player (MVP) in 1963 when he went 25–5. He also threw four no-hitters and led the league in strikeouts four times. Opposing batters often found him untouchable. Former Pirates star Willie Stargell said, "Hitting against Sandy Koufax is like drinking coffee with a fork."

Koufax teamed with **Don Drysdale** to help the Dodgers win three World Series. Drysdale was an intimidating right-hander. He wasn't afraid to pitch inside. He led the league

CONSECUTIVE SEASONS WITH 10+ VICTORIES
DODGERS TEAM RECORD
Don Sutton: 15 (1966–80)

DRYSDALE
53

in hit batters five times. He also won a Cy Young Award and was an eight-time All-Star. Drysdale set a league record by pitching 58 2/3 consecutive scoreless innings in 1968.

That record was broken by another Dodger, **Orel Hershiser**. The lanky right-hander had excellent control. He also could change speeds to baffle hitters. In 1988, Hershiser went 59 straight innings without allowing a run. He was 23–8 that year and won the NL Cy Young Award. Then Hershiser went 3–0 in the postseason. He was named MVP of the NL Championship Series and World Series.

Lefty **Clayton Kershaw** matched Koufax by winning three Cy Young Awards, five NL earned run average (ERA) titles, and the

FERNANDOMANIA

In 1981 rookie pitcher **Fernando Valenzuela** took the league by storm. The 20-year-old lefty threw a league-high eight shutouts. He also led the Dodgers to their first World Series title since 1965. A native of Mexico, Valenzuela became a hero to Latino baseball fans throughout North America.

KERSHAW
22

NL MVP Award. He had a strong fastball and a wicked curve. Kershaw led the Dodgers to the playoffs nine times in 12 years. He and young right-hander **Walker Buehler** were an effective one-two punch as the Dodgers reached the World Series in 2018.

ROBINSON
42

CHAPTER 2
INFIELDERS

No history of the Dodgers—or of baseball itself—would be complete without the story of **Jackie Robinson**. In 1947, Robinson became the first Black player in the major leagues since the 1800s. He also changed the game with his play. Robinson was the NL Rookie of the Year in 1947. Two years later he hit .342 and won the NL batting title and MVP Award. Robinson's courage and ability opened the door for generations of talented Black players to come.

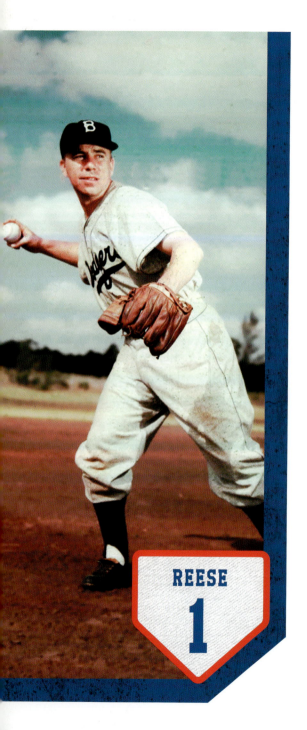

REESE
1

Robinson spent much of his career at second base. He played next to another future Hall of Famer, shortstop **Pee Wee Reese**. The 10-time All-Star was one of the steadiest players in the league. He played his final season in 1958, the Dodgers' first in Los Angeles.

Gil Hodges was another great Brooklyn star who made the move west to LA. The slugging first baseman

HODGES
14

was a consistent power threat for more than a decade. Hodges drove in more than 100 runs in seven straight seasons. He also hit .340 with two home runs in the Dodgers' World Series victories in 1955 and 1959.

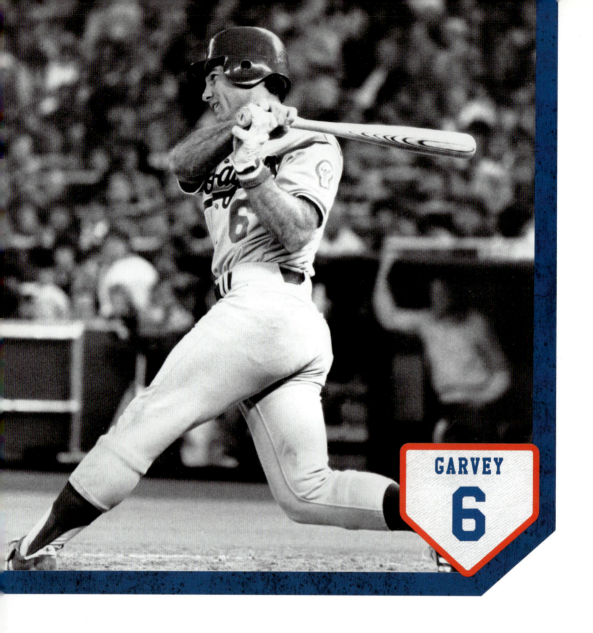

GARVEY
6

In the 1970s, the Dodgers infield was especially strong at the corners. First baseman **Steve Garvey** was the NL MVP in 1974. It was the first of eight straight All-Star seasons for the line-drive hitter. Garvey slugged four home runs in four games as the MVP of the 1978 NL Championship Series. Later, he hit .417 as the Dodgers beat the Yankees in the 1981 World Series.

Across the diamond, **Ron Cey** anchored third base for 10 years. He was nicknamed "Penguin" for his squat stature. Cey averaged more than 20 home runs per year as a Dodger. He also was a six-time All-Star.

UP THE MIDDLE

The Dodgers also had talented middle infielders in the 1970s. Second baseman **Davey Lopes** led the National League in stolen bases in 1975 and 1976. Shortstop **Bill Russell** had a strong glove. He spent 18 seasons with the team. They were both starters along with Garvey in the 1980 All-Star Game at Dodger Stadium.

PIAZZA
31

CHAPTER 3
CATCHERS AND OUTFIELDERS

Catcher **Mike Piazza** came out of nowhere and became an All-Star. He was drafted in the 62nd round in 1988. Then he began a Hall of Fame career with the Dodgers. He hit more home runs than any catcher in MLB history. He was voted the NL Rookie of the Year in 1993, when he hit 35 homers and drove in 112 runs.

Roy Campanella was a former Negro Leagues star. He joined the Dodgers a year after Jackie Robinson's breakthrough. The stocky catcher had tremendous power. Campanella set career highs with 41 homers

CAMPANELLA
39

SNIDER
4

and 142 RBI in 1953. That year he won the second of his three NL MVP Awards.

In the 1950s, the three best center fielders in the game all played in New York. The Yankees had Mickey Mantle. Willie Mays starred for the New York Giants. And **Duke Snider** was slugging home runs in Brooklyn.

Snider hit 40 or more home runs in five straight seasons. And in 1955, Snider had a dream season. He led the major leagues with 136 RBI. Then he hit four home runs as the Dodgers topped the Yankees in the World Series.

Outfielder **Willie Davis** made his debut with the Dodgers in 1960. He played a smooth center field for the next 13 seasons. He helped the team win two World Series. A three-time

BELLINGER
35

20

Gold Glove winner, Davis also led the majors with 16 triples in 1970.

In 2017 **Cody Bellinger** emerged as one of baseball's top young superstars. That year, the NL Rookie of the Year hit 39 homers and drove in 97 runs. But in 2019 he was even better. Bellinger rode his sweet swing to the NL MVP Award. He posted career-high marks of 47 homers, 115 RBI, and a .305 batting average.

TIMELINE

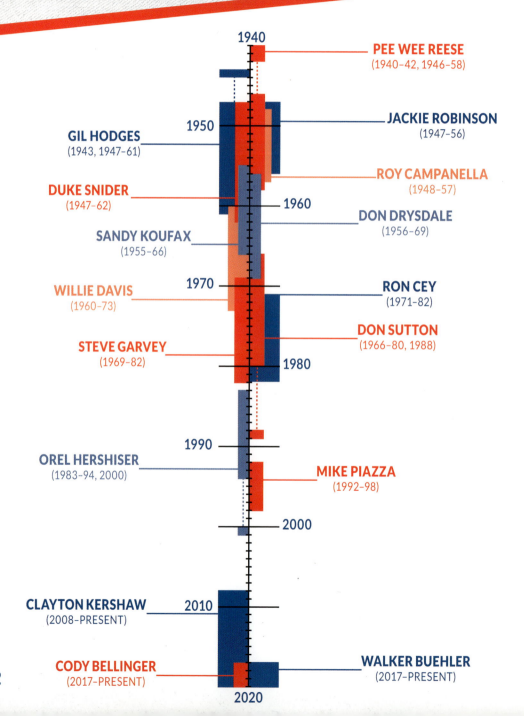

1940

PEE WEE REESE
(1940–42, 1946–58)

1950

JACKIE ROBINSON
(1947–56)

GIL HODGES
(1943, 1947–61)

ROY CAMPANELLA
(1948–57)

DUKE SNIDER
(1947–62)

1960

DON DRYSDALE
(1956–69)

SANDY KOUFAX
(1955–66)

1970

RON CEY
(1971–82)

WILLIE DAVIS
(1960–73)

DON SUTTON
(1966–80, 1988)

STEVE GARVEY
(1969–82)

1980

1990

OREL HERSHISER
(1983–94, 2000)

MIKE PIAZZA
(1992–98)

2000

CLAYTON KERSHAW
(2008–PRESENT)

2010

CODY BELLINGER
(2017–PRESENT)

WALKER BUEHLER
(2017–PRESENT)

2020

TEAM FACTS

LOS ANGELES DODGERS

Formerly: Brooklyn (various nicknames, 1884–1931); Brooklyn Dodgers (1932–57)

World Series titles: 6 (1955, 1959, 1963, 1965, 1981, 1988)*

Key managers:

Walter Alston (1954–76)

2,040–1,613 (.558), 4 World Series titles

Leo Durocher (1938–46, 1948)

738–565 (.566)

Tommy Lasorda (1976–96)

1,599–1,439 (.526), 2 World Series titles

MORE INFORMATION

To learn more about the Los Angeles Dodgers, go to **pressboxbooks.com/AllAccess**.

These links are routinely monitored and updated to provide the most current information available.

*1903 through 2019

GLOSSARY

anchored
Held down.

debut
First appearance.

intimidating
Frightening or threatening.

shutout
A game in which one team does not score.

steadiest
Most consistent, or most able to perform in an expected manner over and over.

stocky
Broad and sturdily built.

INDEX